Ukulele 1

INTRODUCTION

You bought a ukulele...so now what?

Congratulations! You look great holding that new ukulele (even standing in front of the mirror, lip-synching to your favorite songs and swaying back and forth). But won't your friends and family be even more impressed if you can actually play the darn thing? In just a couple of weeks, you'll be playing some very well-known tunes, plus jamming on some new ones.

All we ask is that you observe the three **P**s: **P**atience, **P**ractice and **P**ace yourself.

Don't try to bite off more than you can chew, and DON'T skip ahead. If your fingers hurt, take the day off. If you get frustrated, put it down and come back later. If you forget something, go back and learn it again. If you're having a great time, forget about dinner and keep on playing. Most importantly, have fun!

ABOUT THE AUDIO

*G*lad you noticed the added bonus—audio tracks! All the music examples in this book are included with the audio, so you can hear how they sound first and play along when you're ready. Take a listen whenever you see this symbol: ❶

Each audio example is preceded by count-off "clicks" to help you feel the beat before the music starts. If the tempo (speed) is too fast for you, no problem! The audio is also enhanced with **Playback+** so Mac and PC users can adjust the recording to any tempo without changing the pitch, set loop points, change keys, pan left or right—available exclusively from Hal Leonard!

To access audio visit:
www.halleonard.com/mylibrary
Enter Code
2715-1415-3090-0149

ISBN 978-1-4803-0846-6

HAL•LEONARD®
CORPORATION
7777 W. BLUEMOUND RD. P.O. BOX 13819 MILWAUKEE, WI 53213

In Australia Contact:
Hal Leonard Australia Pty. Ltd.
4 Lentara Court
Cheltenham, Victoria, 3192 Australia
Email: ausadmin@halleonard.com.au

Visit Hal Leonard Online at
www.halleonard.com

A GOOD PLACE TO START

Your ukulele is your friend...

A ukulele can be like a good friend over the years—it'll get you through the rough times and help you sing away the blues. So, before we get started, give your four-stringed friend a name.

What a beauty!

Below is a picture of a soprano ukulele. "Ukes" come in several different sizes, but they all share the same parts. Get acquainted with the parts here, and don't forget to give it a name!

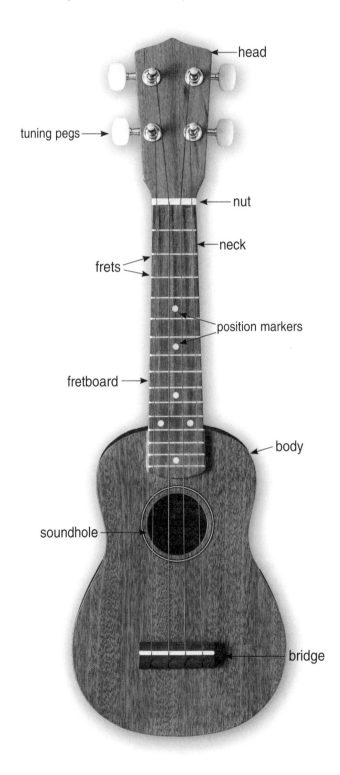

head

tuning pegs

nut

neck

frets

position markers

fretboard

body

soundhole

bridge

TUNING

When you tune, you correct the **pitch** of each string. Pitch refers to how high or low a musical tone is. This is adjusted by tightening (or loosening) the string, using the tuning pegs on the head of the ukulele. The tighter the string, the higher the pitch.

The tuning for a ukulele isn't as standard as it is for guitar and bass, but the most common tuning is called "reentrant tuning," so that's what we'll use in this book. Your four ukulele strings should be tuned to the pitches *G–C–E–A*. Notice that string 4 is actually pitched higher than strings 3 and 2. This is one thing that gives the ukulele its characteristic sound.

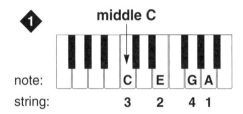

CAUTION: Tighten the strings slowly and not too much, or you'll be heading back to the store to buy new ones!

Piano tuning

No, you aren't about to tune an entire piano! If you have a piano or electronic keyboard nearby, play the above notes one at a time and tune the corresponding uke string until its pitch matches that of the piano.

Electronic tuning

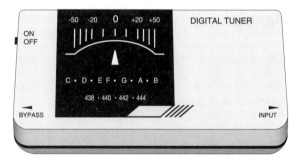

If you don't have a piano or keyboard, you may want to purchase an electronic tuner. A guitar tuner will work, but make sure it's a "chromatic tuner" so it will recognize the pitches of your ukulele's strings.

A tuner will "listen" to each string as you play it and indicate whether the pitch is too high or too low. If you don't have a piano and you can't buy a tuner, don't give up hope—there's yet another solution:

Relative tuning

To tune your ukulele by ear, you must tune the strings to each other. This is done in the following manner:

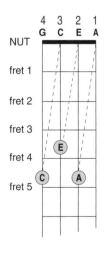

 Assume that string 4 is tuned correctly to G (even if it's not).

 Press string 4 behind fret 5, and play (pluck) the depressed string 4 and the open string 3 together. When they match, you're in tune. String 4 will sound "higher," but the notes are the same. String 4 will be an octave higher than string 3. (Don't worry, we'll explain that later!)

 Press string 3 behind fret 4 and tune the open string 2 to it.

 Press string 2 behind fret 5 and tune the open string 1 to it.

A FEW MORE THINGS
...before we jam!

Sit down and stay a while...

Perhaps the most comfortable and least tiring way to learn ukulele is to sit while playing.

Once you learn a few tunes, feel free to stand up, lie down, hold it behind your head, or whatever. But for now, let's put that extra effort to better use—playing!

sitting

standing

Please hold...

Hold the neck of the ukulele with your **left hand,** with your thumb resting comfortably behind the neck. Hold the neck slightly upward, not downward (at least not until you're on stage in front of thousands of fans).

Most players use either their first finger or thumb on their **right hand** to strum or pluck the strings. You'll get the best sound by strumming where the neck joins the body.

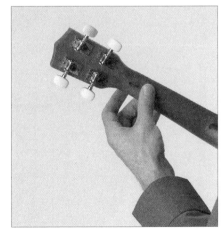

left hand

right hand

There's nothing stressful here, so don't grip the neck too hard. (You might strangle it!)

Picture This...

Fretboard diagrams (or "grids") show a portion of the fretboard (or "fingerboard") and tell you where to play the notes and chords. Circles with note names are drawn onto the diagrams to indicate the notes played.

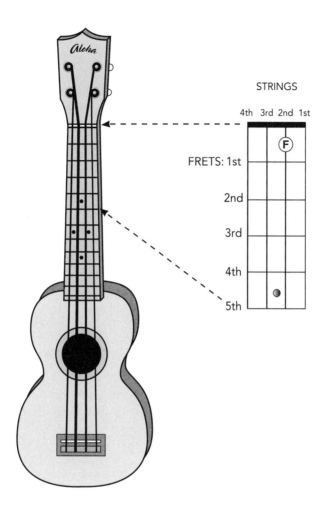

Think of your left-hand fingers as being numbered 1 through 4.

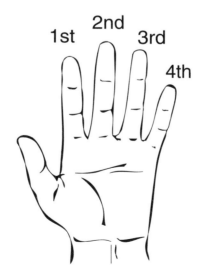

DOG-EAR THESE TWO PAGES
(...you'll need to review them later)

fold

Music is a language with its own symbols, structure and rules (and exceptions to those rules). Reading, writing and playing music requires that you know the symbols and rules. But let's take it one step at a time (a few now, a few later)...

Notes

Music is written with little doo-hickeys called **notes**. They come in many shapes and sizes, but each one has two main characteristics: its **pitch** (indicated by its position on the staff) and its **rhythmic value** (indicated by the following symbols):

whole note   **half note**   **quarter note**

The rhythmic value tells you how many beats the note lasts. Most commonly, a quarter note equals one beat. After that, it's just like fractions. (Yeah, we hate math, too!)

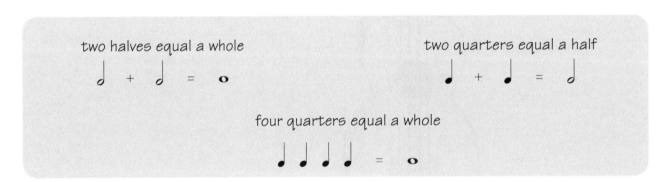

Staff

Notes are positioned on (or near) a **staff**, which consists of five parallel lines and four spaces. (The plural for staff is "staves.") Each line and space represents a different pitch.

Ledger Lines

Since all notes won't fit on just five lines and four spaces, short **ledger lines** are used to temporarily extend the staff:

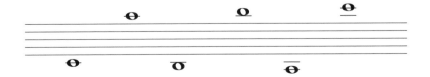

Clef

A funky symbol called a **clef** indicates which pitches are represented on the staff. Music uses a variety of clefs for different instruments, but you only need to learn about one—the **treble clef**.

Treble clef

A treble clef makes the lines and spaces on the staff have the following pitches:

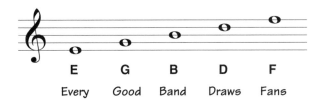

E	G	B	D	F
Every	Good	Band	Draws	Fans

F A C E

"FACE"

An easy way to remember the line pitches (from bottom to top) is "**E**very **G**ood **B**and **D**raws **F**ans." The spaces simply spell the word "**FACE**."

Measures (or Bars)

Notes on a staff are divided into **measures** (or "bars") to help you keep track of where you are in the song. (Imagine reading a book without any periods, commas, or capital letters!)

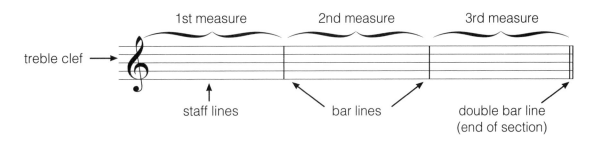

Time Signatures (or Meters)

A **time signature** (or "meter") indicates how the beats in each measure will be counted. It contains two numbers: the top number tells you how many beats will be in each measure, and the bottom number tells you which type of note will equal one beat.

four beats per measure
quarter note (1/4) = one beat

three beats per measure
quarter note (1/4) = one beat

☞   **R**elax for a while, read through all this again later, and then move on.
(Trust us—as you go through the book, you'll start to understand this stuff.)

LESSON 1

Don't just sit there, play something!

We're tuned, relaxed, comfortable, and we're eager to play! Let's get down to business...

As you know from page 4, your left hand "selects" a note by pressing a string at a fret, while your right hand "plays" that string by plucking it. To play a string **open** means to play it without pressing a fret.

String 1: A

Forget the other three strings for now—just focus on string 1. Use the photos and fretboard diagrams to locate your first notes.

Play string 1 open and you will hear A. This note is shown on a grid and staff like this:

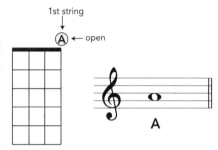

Play string 1 while pressing fret 2 with finger 2 and you will hear B.

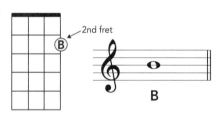

Press fret 3 with finger 3 to play C. (You can even leave your second finger on fret 2 if you'd like.)

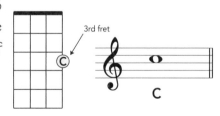

☞   "**W**ait a minute! What about fret 1?" Good question!
That note is called B-flat, but we'll explain flats later. For now, ignorance is bliss!

Put it to good use...

Three notes in about three minutes—not bad for a beginner! Practice these three notes again and again using the following tunes. Pluck the strings with either your first finger or your thumb. You can even switch between them if you'd like. (We won't tell!) If you need a review of rhythmic values or time signatures, turn back to pages 6 and 7.

❷ A–B–C

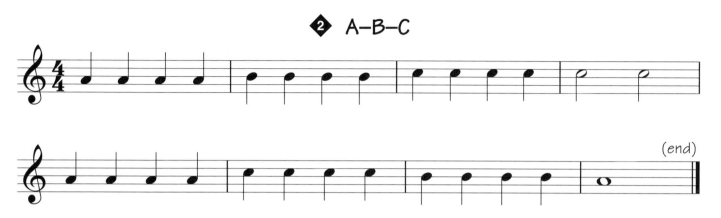

(end)

Just like reading a book, go to the next line in the song as soon as you reach the end of each staff. However, when you see this symbol (▤), the song is over.

❸ First Song

☞ **Fingering Tip #1:** When pressing a fret, use only your fingertip (not your whole finger), so you don't accidentally touch other strings.

❹ Rockin' the A String

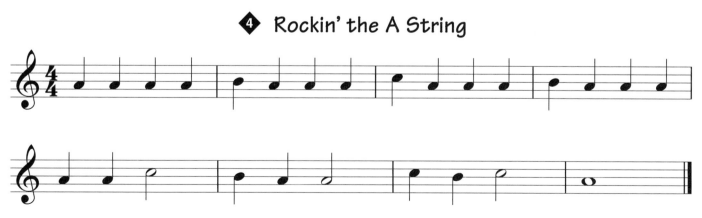

Don't be afraid to repeat these tunes over and over, playing them a little faster each time. When you feel confident with the notes (and after you've grabbed a snack from the fridge), meet us back here for Lesson 2.

LESSON 2

Moving on...

Welcome back! Now you know three notes and three songs. Ok, we admit the songs were boring, so let's learn three more notes and some better songs.

HELPFUL HINT: Take a few seconds to flip back to page 3 and make sure your uke is still in tune. (If the dog starts howling, it probably isn't!)

String 2: E

We'll learn string 2 almost the same way we learned string 1. But this time, we'll skip fret 2 instead of fret 1.

Play string 2 open. That's E, which is located on the bottom staff line.

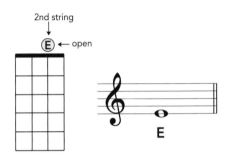

Play string 2 while pressing fret 1 with finger 1 and you get F, which sits in the bottom space of the staff.

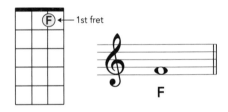

Press fret 3 with finger 3 and you have G.

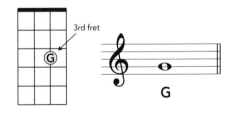

☞ "Why did we skip fret 2?" That note is F-sharp.
We won't ignore your questions forever—you'll learn about sharps and flats in Lesson 3.

You know the drill—let's put these new notes to use!

Practice your new notes with this short exercise:

❺ E–F–G

Now, let's check out some tunes (better ones, we might add) that use all six notes you've learned so far. If you need to, feel free to review A, B and C first. (We'll wait!)

❻ Uke Blues

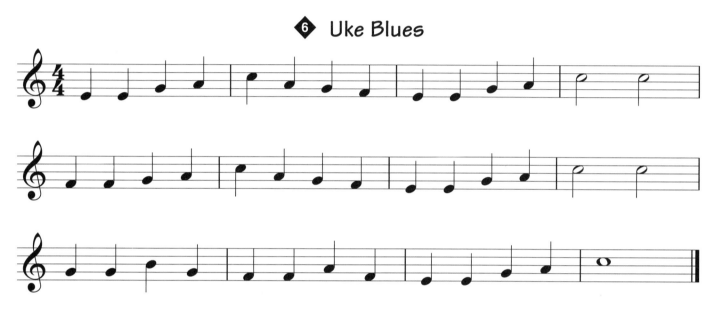

☞ **Fingering Tip #2:** When changing fingers from string 1 to string 2 (or vice versa), try to let your eyes move ahead in the music and move the correct finger to the correct string before the next note occurs.

In this next example, "*grad. accel.*" stands for *gradual accelerando*. That's a fancy music term that simply means to gradually speed up. You'll sound just like the organist at the baseball stadium!

❼ Bleacher Rock

grad. accel.

8 Beach Blues

Fingering Tip #3: When moving from one fret on one string to the same fret on a string below it, just "roll" your finger down to play the second note. In the following song, for example, play the G on string 2 with your third finger and then flatten it to play the C on string 1. It might not look all that pretty, but it gets a smooth sound!

9 Open Fields

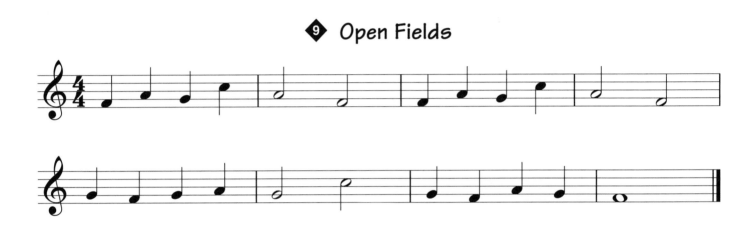

Pay close attention to your timing in this next song. Try to make sure you're not rushing or dragging—each note should fall right on the beat!

10 Pachelbel's Canon

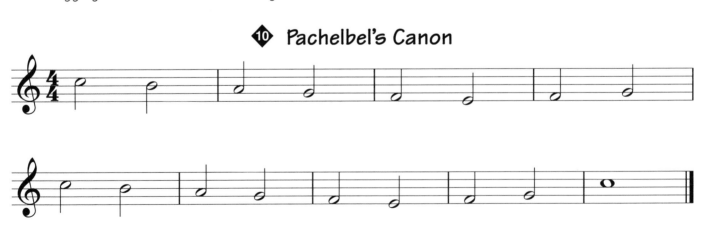

If your fingertips hurt, you can take a break. But never fear—the more you practice, the quicker they'll toughen up. (No pain, no gain, right?)

MORE NOTES ON MUSIC

Pardon the pun...

Before we start Lesson 3, we need to tell you more about the hieroglyphics of music.

> ### Rests
>
> A musical **rest** is a pause. Rests are like notes in that they have their own rhythmic values, instructing the musician how long (or how many beats) to pause:
>
> | whole rest | half rest | quarter rest |
> |:---:|:---:|:---:|
> | (four beats) | (two beats) | (one beat) |

During a rest, mute the strings by lightly touching them with your strumming hand. In the following 4/4 example, you'll play: E, E, pause, E, pause, pause, pause, pause, E, E, pause, pause, E, pause, pause, E.

⓫ Take a Breather

IMPORTANT: A rest symbol does not mean to rest your fingers or put down the ukulele! Rests are opportunities to get your fingers (and your brain) ready for the next set of notes.

⓬ Counting the Breakers

 Ok, we realize that playing is more fun than resting, but the rests in a song are just as important as the notes. Don't skip over them!

LESSON 3

Third time's a charm...

Unbelievable—you've learned six notes already! At this rate, you'll have the entire fretboard memorized in a few days. (Ok, maybe not.) How 'bout another string? Make sure you're still in tune first. If not, hit page 3 again.

String 3: C

For string 3, you only need to learn two notes for now. (You're welcome!)

 Play string 3 open. That's C, which is written on the first ledger line below the staff.

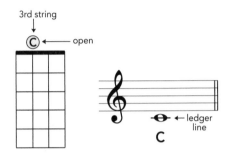

 Play string 3 while pressing fret 2 with finger 2 and you get D.

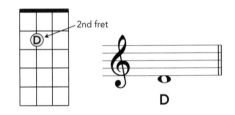

☞ You're right—you already learned a C on page 8. Since the musical alphabet only uses the letters A through G, this type of repetition will eventually occur with all the note names. The first C you learned sounds one **octave** higher than this new C. An octave refers to pitches that are eight note names apart.

Let's practice these two new notes. This tune is a bit boring (how exciting can it be with only two notes?), but you still need to watch out for those pesky rests!

⑬ Two-Note Jam

CAUTION: Don't move on to the next page until you feel like you've mastered these two notes...

14 Short'nin' Bread

15 Aura Lee

Put the ukulele down for a minute and try reciting the note names in the next song. Then practice locating the notes on the fretboard before playing them. Have fun with it!

16 She'll Be Strummin' 'Round the Mountain

Alright, that's enough work for today. Get some sleep, eat a good breakfast, and we'll meet you back here tomorrow. Start off by reviewing Lessons 1, 2 and 3 before moving ahead.

YOU'RE LOOKING SHARP!

Music is made up of intervals called **half steps** and **whole steps**. Each fret on the ukulele equals one half step, and a whole step equals two half steps.

When a song requires a note to move only a half step higher or lower, a special symbol is placed in front (to the left) of that note. It's called an **accidental**. Watch out—they can cause accidents while playing! Here are two types of accidentals:

One half step higher is called a **sharp** and looks like a tic-tac-toe board: ♯

One half step lower is called a **flat** and looks like a lowercase "b" that's trying to suck in its gut: ♭

EXCEPTIONS TO THE RULE (Bummer!): From E to F is only a half step, and from B to C is only a half step.

Since you only got two notes on page 14...

We'll give you not one, but two new notes! How 'bout one sharp and one flat? Let's return to strings 1 and 2 and check 'em out!

On string 1, press fret 1 with finger 1 and you'll hear B♭.

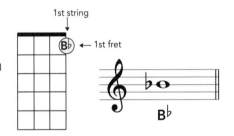

On string 2, press fret 2 with finger 2 and you'll hear F♯.

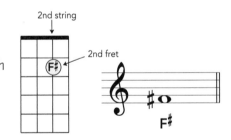

Try out this exercise to get some practice with your new sharp note. But don't cut yourself! (Sorry, couldn't resist...)

🔷 I Know a Sharp

Remember to say the note names aloud first and locate them on the fretboard before playing so you don't fall...uh..."flat" on your face. (Sorry again...)

18 Flat-Out Rockin'

19 This Old Uke

☞ A **natural** sign (♮) cancels a sharp or flat, returning the note to its natural pitch.

20 Uke Holmes: Private Eye

☞ **IMPORTANT:** An accidental lasts for an entire measure, as in the third measure above. It automatically goes back to normal in the next bar, unless you see another accidental there.

LESSON 4

Lower, but higher?

Progress report: three strings and ten notes! It's like a bag of potato chips—you just can't stop, can you? Well then, it's time to learn the last string...

String 4: G

This is where things get weird on the uke (for soprano and concert sizes, anyway). Because of the unique reentrant tuning, string 4 (G) is actually pitched higher than string 3. As a matter of fact, it's even higher than string 2! Because of this, string 4 is mainly used when playing chords (coming up soon), but we might as well learn a couple of notes on it while we're here. It won't bite, we promise!

Playing string 4 open is G, which is written on the second line of the staff.

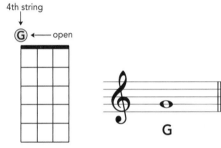

Playing fret 2 with finger 2 is A, which looks like this on a grid and staff:

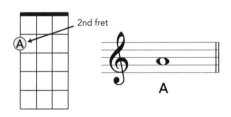

㉑ G–A

Guess what? You've already learned both of these notes on other strings—the same pitches and everything! Play this next tune on string 4 first, and then play it again using strings 1 and 2 instead. (If you need a quick review, go back to pages 8 and 10.)

㉒ More Than One Way to Skin a Cat

Enough of that...let's jam!

Play the following example using your new notes on string 4.

㉓ Wind Chimes

Now, let's get ambitious and work through all four strings! Are you up for it? (You might need a snack first...)

㉔ Blue Water

☞ FRIENDLY REMINDER: The next song is in 3/4 meter, which means there are three beats (quarter notes) per measure. If you're scratching your head, flip back to page 7 for a review.

㉕ Amazing Grace

Wow, you're doing great! Now it's time to dig a little deeper into rhythms...

RHYTHM TALK

Can you spare a quarter? How about an eighth?

An **eighth note** has a flag on it: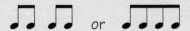

Two eighth notes equal one quarter note (or one beat is 4/4 and 3/4). To make it easier on the eyes, eighth notes are connected with a beam, like this:

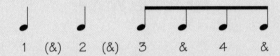

To count eighth notes, divide the beat in half and say "and" between the beats:

Practice this by first counting out loud while tapping your foot on the beat.
Then play the notes while counting and tapping. How's that for multi-tasking?

What about the eighth rest?

Good question—glad you're paying attention! An eighth rest looks like this: ⅂
Eighth rests are just like eighth notes, but you... pause instead of playing a note.
Count, tap, play and pause with the following example:

Let's try out those brand-new, shiny eighth notes, shall we? (Keep that foot tapping!)

26 Rockin' Riff

Excellent work! But why stop there?

Pickups aren't just trucks...

Instead of starting a song with rests, a **pickup measure** can be used. It simply deletes the rests that would normally appear before the first note. So, if a pickup measure only includes one beat, you should count "1, 2, 3" and start playing on beat 4.

Let's see a pickup measure in action:

27 Snake Charmer

28 Brahms' Lullaby
(Try not to fall asleep during this one...)

Fantastic! Play these tunes again and again until you've mastered them. You haven't forgotten the three Ps, have you? **P**atience, **P**ractice and **P**ace yourself!

More Accidentals...

Let's add two more notes: B-flat on string 4 and E-flat on string 3.

On string 4, play fret 3 with finger 3 and you get B-flat. (You learned this note earlier on string 1.)

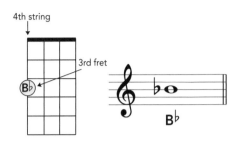

On string 3, play fret 3 with finger 3 and you get E-flat. (This note can also be called D-sharp.)

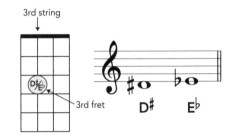

29 Motherless Uke

REMEMBER: A **natural** sign (♮) cancels out a previous sharp or flat, returning the note to its natural pitch.

30 Bach Rock

MORE RHYTHM TALK

Nice tie!

A **tie** connects two notes and tells you to extend the first note to the end of the second note:

1 2 3 (4 1) (2) 3 (4 1 2) 3 4

Always count out loud until you begin to think and feel the beat automatically.

Dotted notes—what's the "point"?

Another way to extend the length of a note is with a **dot**. A dot extends the note by half of its value. (See, those math classes came in handy after all!) Most common is the **dotted half note**:

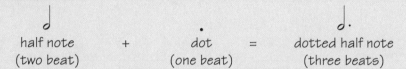

half note	+	dot	=	dotted half note
(two beat)		(one beat)		(three beats)

You'll find dotted half notes in many songs—especially in 3/4 meter.

③① Greenstrings

WARNING: If you haven't slept since page 1, continuing could be hazardous to your enjoyment of learning the ukulele. Get some sleep!

The next song includes **dotted quarter notes**, which get one and a half beats:

quarter note   +   dot   =   dotted quarter note
(1 beat)   (1/2 beat)   (1 1/2 beats)

Listen to audio track 32 while clapping on the beats. Can you feel the rhythm of the dotted quarter notes? Now try playing it…

32 Michael, Row the Boat Ashore

☞   **Repeat signs** (𝄆———————𝄇) tell you to… wait for it… **repeat** everything between them. If only one sign appears (𝄇), repeat from the beginning of the song.

Let's check out two examples for your plucking pleasure:

33 Hard-Rockin' Riff

34 Motown Riff

And now, the moment you've been waiting for…

LESSON 5
Chords and Tab

You've worked your way through all four strings (quite admirably, we might add), and you've already learned...drum roll, please...14 notes! Now it's time to let your fingers work together to play several notes at once.

Chords

A **chord** consists of three or more notes played simultaneously. Chords are actually more common on uke than single notes and melodies, but knowing the notes (which you now do) will help your understanding of chords. Plus, you can show off all the cool melodies you can play to your friends!

Tablature (or Tab)

Tablature (or "tab") is a staff specifically designed for guitar, bass, and yes...even ukulele. The four lines on a tab staff represent (you guessed it!) the four strings on your uke. The number indicates which fret to press on a particular string. A zero means to play the string open.

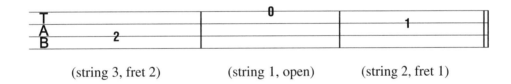

(string 3, fret 2)   (string 1, open)   (string 2, fret 1)

IMPORTANT: Tab should only be used as a guide. You should still observe the time signatures, notes and rhythmic values written on the music staff.

Chord symbols appear above the music staff, indicating which chords to play. Let's dive right in and learn a few of the most common **major** (we'll explain this later) chords on the uke.

C Chord

The C chord is really easy and sounds great—you only need one finger! Place your third finger on fret 3 of string 1, and then strum ALL the strings from 4 to 1, down toward the floor.

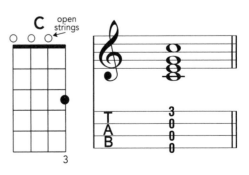

F Chord

For an F chord, place your second finger on fret 2 of string 4 and your first finger on fret 1 of string 2.

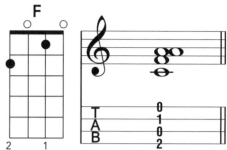

Since you're doing so well, let's learn a G chord!

G Chord

Place your first finger on fret 2 of string 3, your third finger on fret 3 of string 2, and your second finger on fret 2 of string 1.

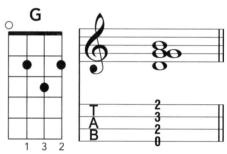

☞ Just like single notes, chords have rhythmic values. For example, a half-note chord gets one strum and lasts for two beats.

◆35 Chord Practice

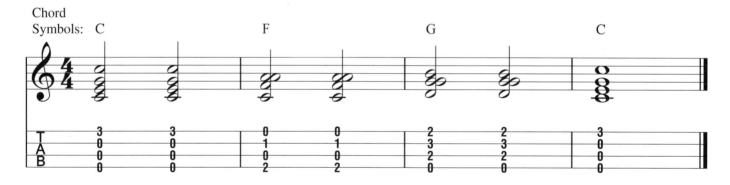

☞ HELPFUL HINT: If your chords sound bad, you're probably muting or muffling a string or two by accident. Play each string one at a time to find the culprit. Then adjust your finger(s) to produce a nice, clean sound.

Chords often follow patterns called **chord progressions**. Here's a chord progression using C, F and G chords.

36 A Logical Progression

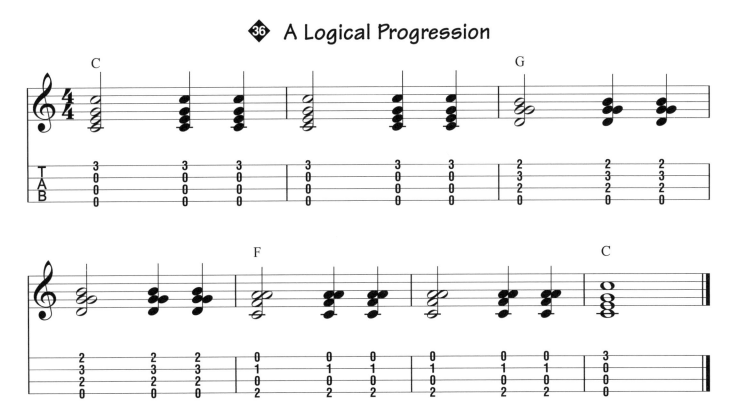

This next chord progression is used in several classic rock songs, including "Louie, Louie" and "Wild Thing."

37 Three-Chord Cliché

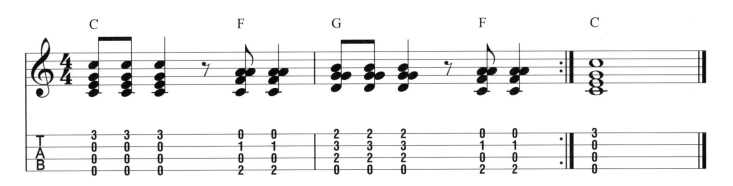

☞ If you're having trouble keeping up with the audio tracks, you can slow them down using the Playback+ audio player. Likewise, if you want to practice something faster, you can speed it up!

Play the following songs by reading **only the chord symbols**. (Some of the melody notes don't exist on most ukes anyway!) Strum once on each beat and sing along with the melody. Go on, don't be shy! Just pretend you're in the shower.

38 Good Night, My Fans

Good night, my fans. Good night, my fans.

Good night, my fans. I'm going to leave you now.

39 Worried Man Blues

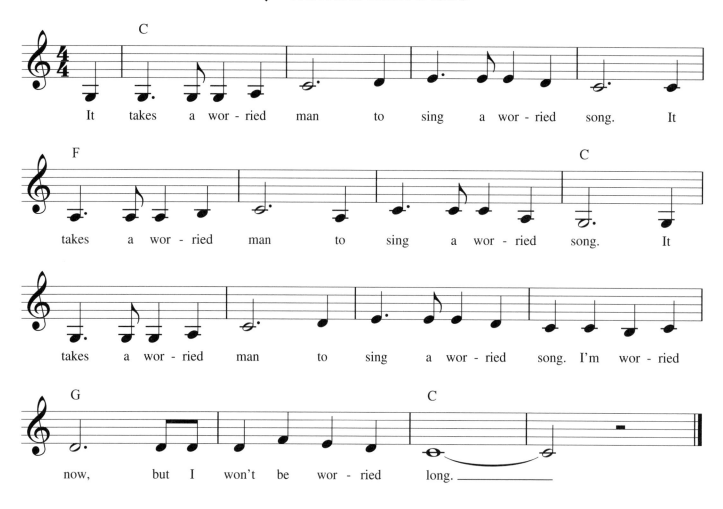

It takes a wor - ried man to sing a wor - ried song. It

takes a wor - ried man to sing a wor - ried song. It

takes a wor - ried man to sing a wor - ried song. I'm wor - ried

now, but I won't be wor - ried long. _____

Great job! Now, play them again and experiment with varying the number of strums per measure. For example, try a half note followed by two quarter notes. Or try three quarter notes followed by two eighth notes. Mix it up and have fun—just remember to keep your foot tapping!

LESSON 6

More Chords...

C7 Chord

To play C7, simply place your first finger on fret 1 of string 1.

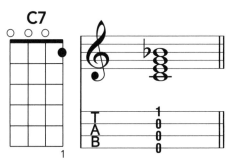

C7 is a **dominant seventh** chord. It's not as intimidating as the name sounds—you just played it with one finger! While a major chord sounds happy and bright, a dominant seventh chord sounds a bit bluesy.

G7 Chord

To play G7, put your second finger on fret 2 of string 3, your first finger on fret 1 of string 2, and your third finger on fret 2 of string 1.

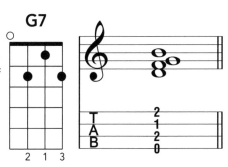

Listen to how dominant seventh chords create a stronger "push" toward the final chord in the next two examples:

40 Seventh Chord Stomp

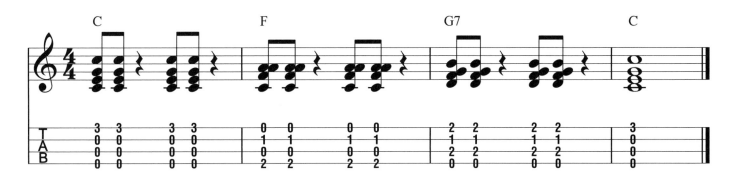

29

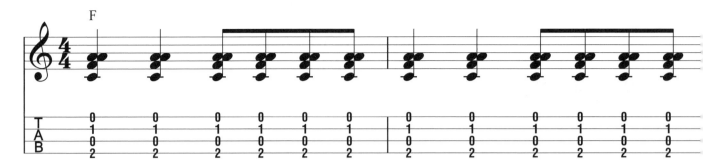

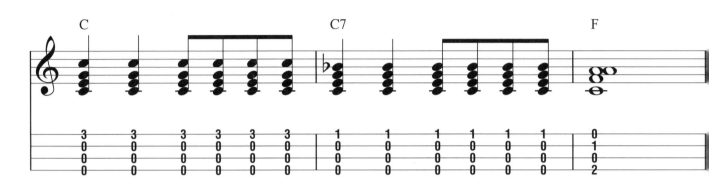

Even More Chords!

Let's look at two more common uke chords to expand your horizons. After all, the more chords you know, the more songs you can play!

A Chord

A is another easy one. Put your second finger on fret 2 of string 4 and your first finger on fret 1 of string 3. Strum, savor, and repeat.

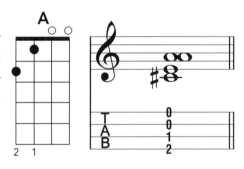

D Chord

The D chord can be tricky. It would be really easy if ukuleles weren't so small, but three fingers can get pretty cramped in such tight quarters. Different people play this chord different ways. Try this to start with and see how you like it:

Put your second finger on string 4, third finger on string 3, and fourth finger on string 2—all on the second fret. Feel free to try the alternate fingerings shown under the grid.

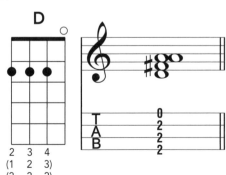

Listen to these chords on the audio and then play along.

42 Chord Tracks #1

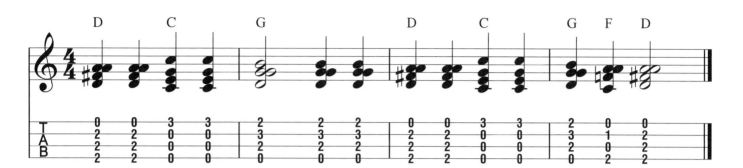

In the next example, try using **upstrums** (↑) for the eighth notes that fall between the beats (on "and"). Simply strum from string 1 to string 4, up toward your face.

43 Chord Tracks #2

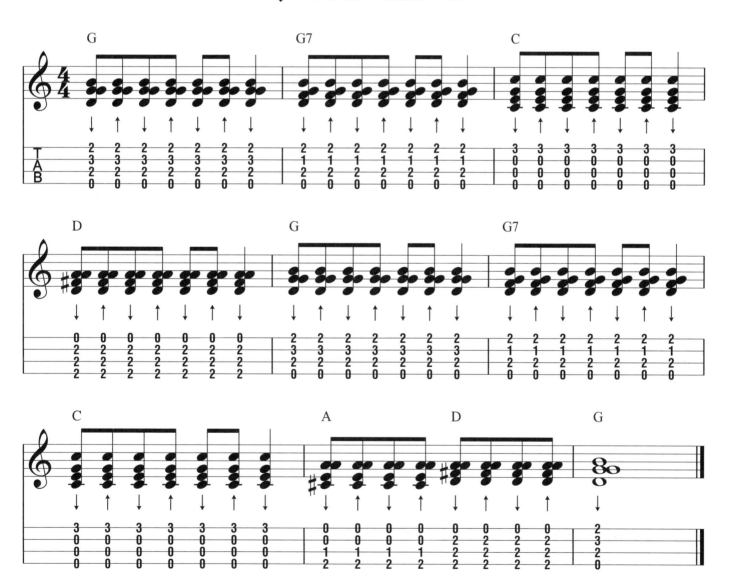

Time for a break! Grab a bite, maybe watch that TV show you recorded earlier... Then come back and practice those chord changes again.

Just like shuffling a deck of cards…

Ok, so it's really not much like that at all, but the **shuffle feel** (or "swing feel") is too important to leave out. When you play with a shuffle feel, the eighth notes are lopsided—the first one is longer than the second. We could get all mathematical about it and explain how you divide the beat into three equal parts, and the first eighth note occupies the space of the first two parts, while the second occupies the space of the last part… Whoa, we lost you there, didn't we? Sorry, never mind.

It's easier to just hear an example, because you already know the sound. You've heard it in literally hundreds of songs—especially blues and country tunes. Listen to Track 44 to hear the difference. First, you'll hear two measures played with a "straight" feel (normal eighth notes). Then you'll hear the same two measures played with a shuffle feel (with "swung" eighth notes).

44

See? We told you you'd recognize it! When you see this symbol (♫ = ♩♪) at the beginning of a song, it means that you should play it with a shuffle or swing feel.

Practice playing with a shuffle feel in this song. Don't forget to use upstrums for the "short" eighth notes that fall between the beats. Your wrist will thank you!

45 Island Shuffle

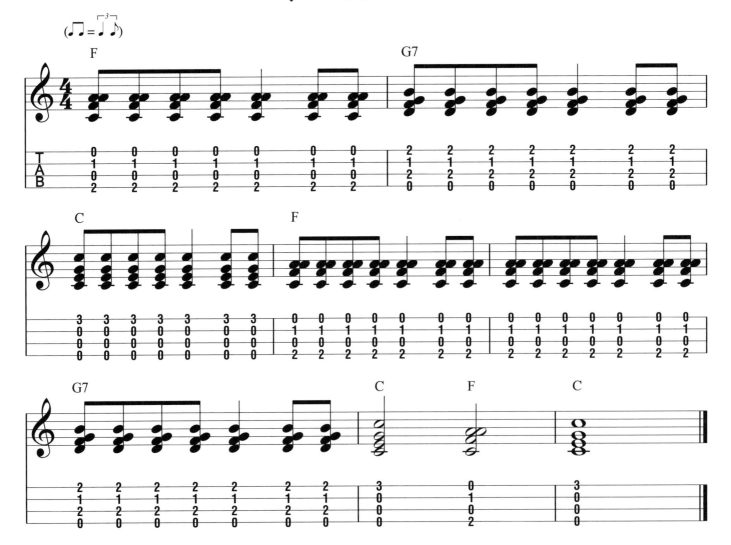

LESSON 7

It's just a minor thing, really...

Major chords sound happy, but **minor** chords sound sad or dark.

A **chord suffix** tells you what type of chord it is. If a chord name is just a letter by itself (such as C, F and G), you can assume it's a major chord. However, if you see a lowercase "m" after the chord name, it's a minor chord. You've already learned another chord suffix on page 29: dominant seventh (7). But we digress...let's get back to minor chords.

Am Chord

The easiest minor chord is Am. (Don't you love these one-finger chords?)

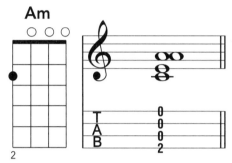

Dm Chord

This one uses three fingers, but it's easier than D major!

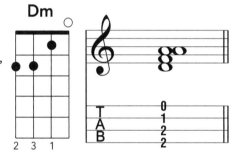

☞ **Fingering Tip #4:** In the chord diagrams above, notice that both Am and Dm use the second finger on string 4, fret 2. This means that you don't even need to pick it up when changing between these two chords. It's not laziness—it's brilliance! The concept is called a **common tone**, and it results in a smoother transition between chords. Keep an eye out for this handy trick in other chord progressions, too!

Check out how easy it is to move back and forth between Am and Dm:

🔷46 More Chord Practice

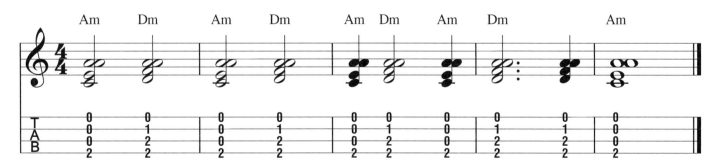

Many songs use a combination of major, minor and dominant seventh chords, as in the following examples:

47 Mixin' It Up #1

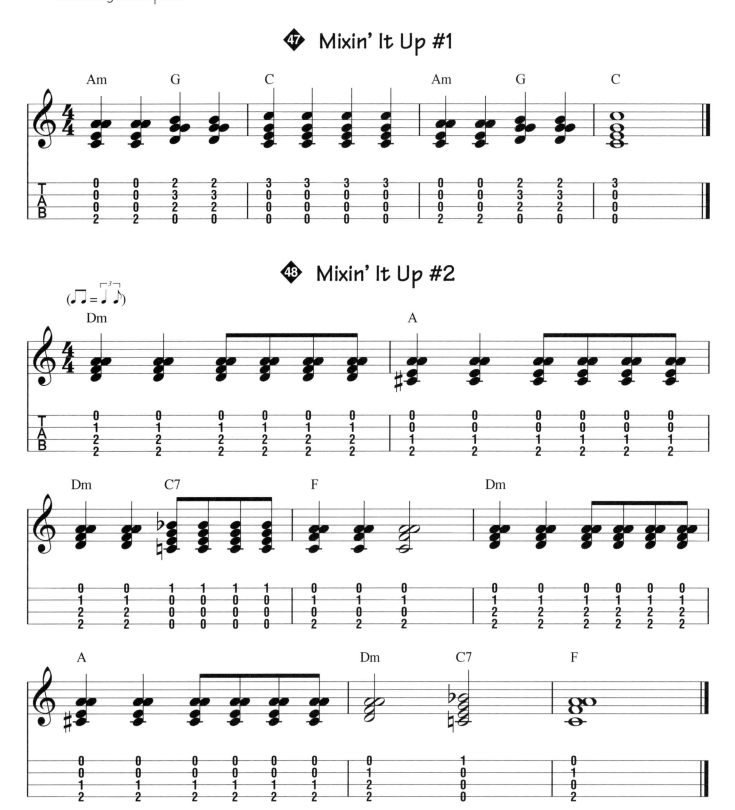

48 Mixin' It Up #2

☞ **REMEMBER:** Use upstrums for eighth notes that fall between the beats!

Em Chord

We'll venture into new territory (fret 4) for this chord, but it's still fairly easy to play.

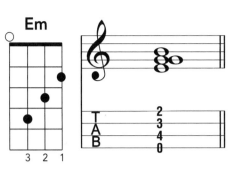

Gm Chord

Notice how the G minor chord is only one note different from the G major chord. The same can be said for D minor/D major and A minor/A major.

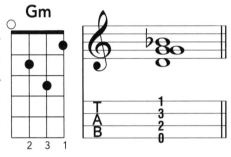

Despite the name, major chords aren't more important than minor chords—they just sound different, that's all.

 Sometimes, music is written in **slash notation**. (It's easier, so why not?) Strum once every time you see a " / " symbol. On the repeat, try adding some upstrums between the beats to mix things up.

49 Mixin' It Up #3

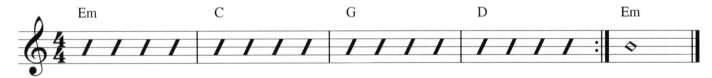

50 Mixin' It Up #4

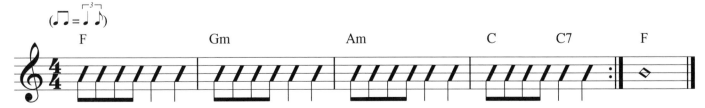

Strum the chords in these next two songs and sing along with the melody.

51 When Johnny Comes Surfing Home

When John - ny comes surf - ing home a - gain, hur - rah, _____ hur - rah! _____ We'll give him a heart - y wel - come then, hur - rah, _____ hur - rah! _____ The fans will cheer and the fans will shout. The clouds will part and the sun will come out. And we'll all feel great when John - ny comes surf - ing home. _____

52 Scarborough Fair

Are you go - ing to Scar - bor - ough Fair? Pars - ley, sage, rose - mar - y and thyme. Re - mem - ber me to one who lives there. _ Once she was a true love of mine.

LESSON 8

Just a few more notes...

Let's fill in some gaps in the already-impressive list of notes you have under your fingers:

 Put your first finger on fret 1 of string 3 to play C-sharp. (This note is part of the A chord, in case you didn't notice.)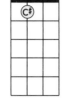

 To play G-sharp, use your fourth finger (yep, the pinky!) on fret 4 of string 2.

 To play a high C-sharp, use your fourth finger on fret 4 of string 1.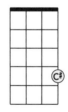

 And finally, stretch that pinky up one more fret on string 1 to play a high D on fret 5.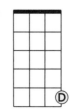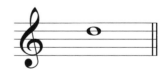

Now, let's take your "sharp" new notes out for a spin! Before you freak out on the very first note, D-sharp is just another name for E-flat, which you learned on page 22. Go back and review it if needed.

53 Danny Boy

(D♯ is the same as E♭)

54 Auld Lang Syne

☞ Time for another break—you've earned it! How 'bout taking the dog for a walk?

LESSON 9

Barre Chords

All the chords you've learned so far have been **open**, meaning that one or more strings are left open. With **barre chords** (pronounced like "bar"), your first finger lays flat across more than one string on the same fret. Barre chords contain no open strings, which makes them **moveable**. (You'll see the beauty of this in a minute...)

B♭ Chord

Place your third finger on fret 3 of string 4, your second finger on fret 2 of string 3, and then lay your first finger flat across strings 2 and 1 at fret 1. It may be uncomfortable at first, but you'll get used to it.

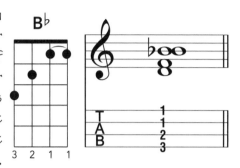

B Chord

Does this shape look familiar? That's right—to play a B chord, all you have to do is slide the B♭ chord shape up one fret. Now you've harnessed the power of a moveable chord shape!

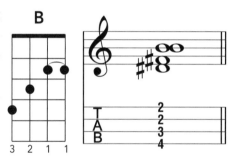

55 Movin' It Up

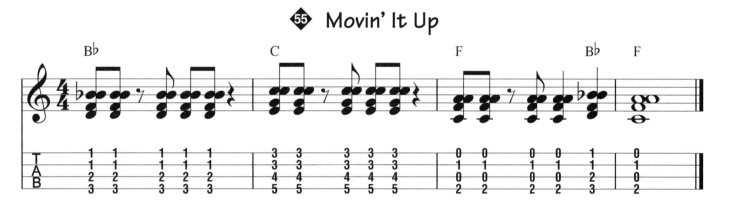

This barre chord shape is sometimes called the **A-form shape** because it's derived from the open A chord. (Play an A chord using fingers 3 and 2 instead of 2 and 1, and you'll see what we mean.) You can play major chords all the way up the neck this way—until your fingers get too crowded, anyway!

Let's put this shape to use in another example—this time as a B chord:

56 "B" Is for Barre Chord

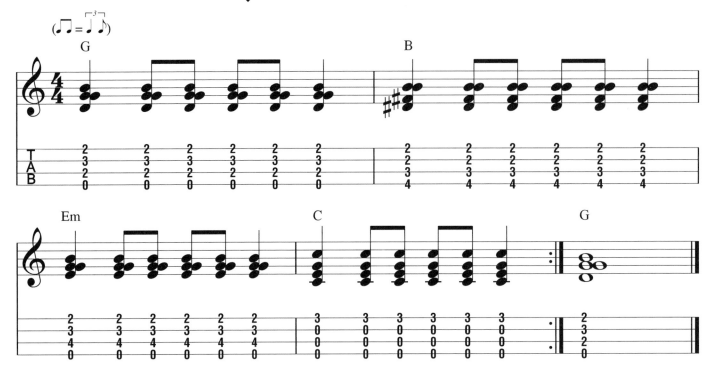

Now, shift gears and think about the open Am chord. There's a barre chord shape derived from that as well:

Bm Chord

Playing the Am shape at the second fret gives you a Bm chord. You'll need to "barre" across strings 3, 2 and 1 with your first finger for this one. Make sure your finger presses all three strings firmly to get a clear sound.

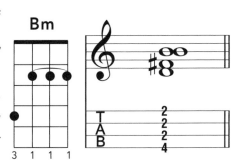

57 A "Barre" Suitable for Minors

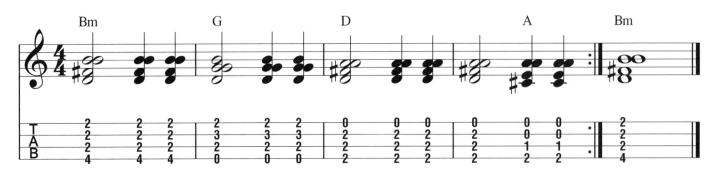

Don't stop now—you're on a roll! Let's learn some more barre chord forms:

E Chord

This one is based on the open Db shape. Technically, it's not a barre chord since you're not barring anything, but we're including it here because it's moveable. (Who gets hung up on technicalities anyway?)

E

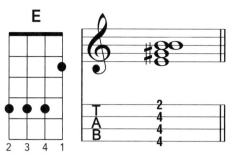

Em Chord (Alternate)

Here's a moveable shape for the open Em chord you learned back on page 35. It's based on the open Dm chord.

Em

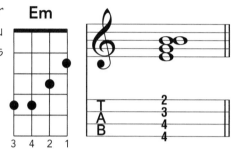

58 Minor Variation

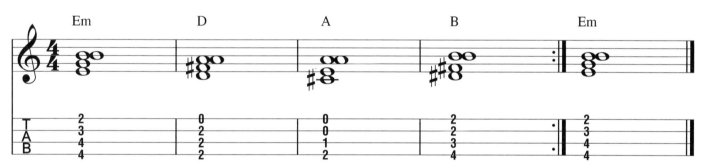

D Chord (Alternate)

Finally! An alternative to that pesky D chord comes along, and you have barre chords to thank for it! This shape is based on the open C chord, and it's one of the easiest barre forms of all.

D

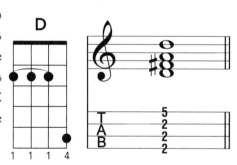

G Chord (Alternate)

The open G chord is easy enough, but here's a barred version that comes in handy for playing other chords like Gb and Ab.

G

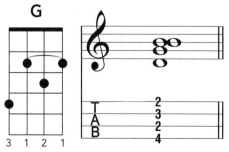

It's not hard to switch quickly between the alternate D and G chords. Just leave your first finger barred across all four strings at fret 2 the whole time.

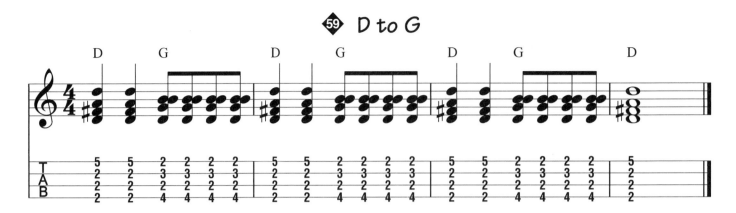

Let's combine several of the forms you've learned so far. Make sure you're properly hydrated first!

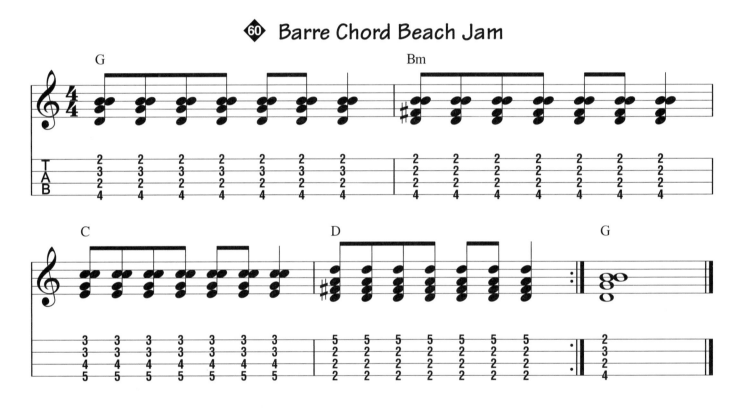

HELPFUL HINT: To switch from the alternate G chord
to the Bm chord, all you have to do is lift finger 2!

D7 Chord

This barre form is based on the open C7 chord. It's another easy one that's extremely useful.

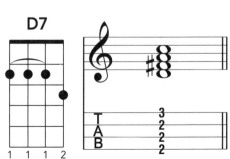

A7 Chord

Before you learn the next barre form, we need to backtrack a bit and show you one more open chord: A7. It's another one-finger wonder chord!

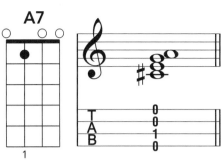

C7 Chord (Alternate)

Now, here's a barre chord that's based on A7:

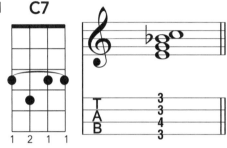

⑥① Mixin' It Up #5

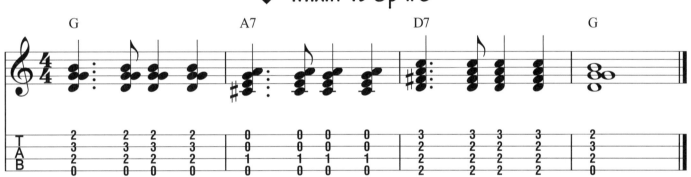

⑥② Mixin' It Up #6

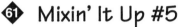

LESSON 10

Take it on the road!

This isn't really a Lesson…it's a jam session!

Two of these songs ("Unplugged Ballad" and "Billy B. Badd") appear at the end of all the other **FastTrack** books (guitar, keyboard, bass, drums, saxophone, harmonica and lead singer). So what, you ask? Well, if you start a band with some friends, you'll already have two songs to play together!

63 64 Sand in My Uke
full band · minus ukulele

65 66 Unplugged Ballad

full band minus ukulele

A Intro

Moderately slow

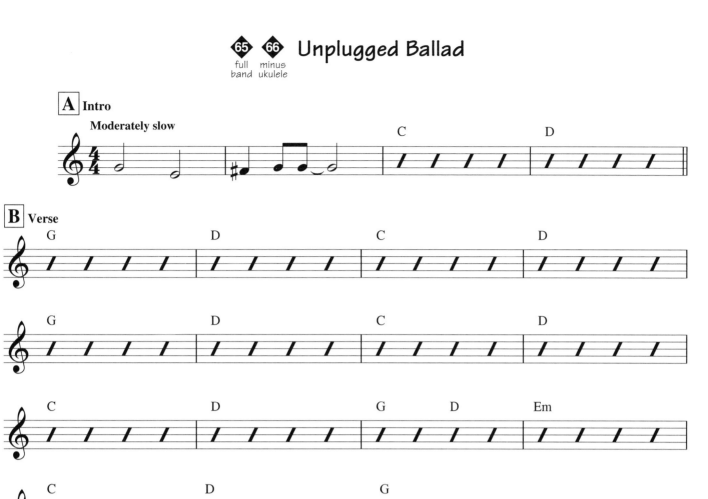

B Verse

C Bridge

D Outro

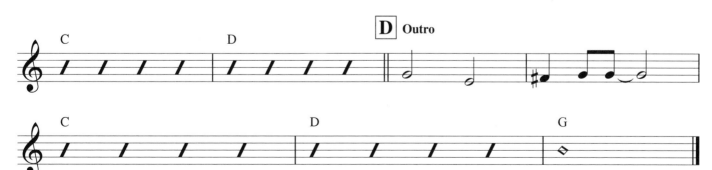

Billy B. Badd

Bravo! Encore!

Remember to practice often and always try to learn more about your instrument.

WAIT! DON'T GO YET!

Even though we hope (and expect) that you'll review the entire book from time to time, we thought you might like a "cheat sheet" that shows all the notes and chords you've learned. Wow, it's impressive to see everything all in one place! Way to go!

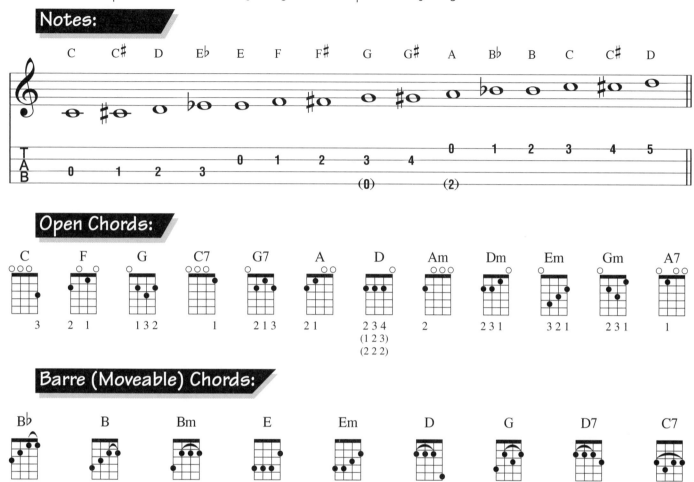

Where to go from here...

Finally, we'd like to offer a few suggestions as you continue on your journey to master the ukulele:

1. **Repetition is the best way to learn.** Review the exercises in this book again and again until you can play all the notes and chords without even thinking about them.

2. **Buy Hal Leonard's *Ukulele Chord Finder*,** which shows you how to play over 1,000 ukulele chords for all occasions. (HL00695802 or HL00695903)

3. **Buy Hal Leonard's *Ukulele Scale Finder*,** which shows you over 1,300 scales on the instrument. (HL00696378)

4. **Buy Hal Leonard's *Easy Songs for Ukulele*,** which includes classic songs from the Beatles, Elvis, Simon & Garfunkel, and more! (HL00695904 or HL00695905)

5. **Enjoy what you do.** Whether it's practicing, jamming, performing, tuning, or even just cleaning your uke, do it with a smile on your face. Life's too short!

See you next time...

SONG INDEX

(...what book would be complete without one?)